D1058894

International Cooking Collection

Entertaining

International
Cooking Collection

Entertaining

Roz Denny

CONTENTS

Published exclusively for Cupress (Canada) Ltd
20 Torbay Road, Markham, Ontario L3R 1G6, Canada
by Woodhead-Faulkner (Publishers) Ltd, Simon & Schuster International Group

This edition first published 1988
© Woodhead-Faulkner (Publishers) Ltd 1988
All rights reserved
ISBN 0-920691-62-5
Printed and bound in Italy

INTRODUCTION

Entertaining can be fun for some—and nerve-wracking for others! There are those who like to spend a long time preparing a meal, paying great attention to detail—while others prefer the quicker more casual approach.

For novice entertainers, I strongly advise learning the art of entertaining gradually—start with just two guests and a simple meal, then increase your guest list and repertoire as your skill improves.

Organization is essential if you wish to spend most of your time with your guests. Prepare vegetables, salads and garnishes beforehand, storing them in the refrigerator to cook or serve at the last minute. Set the table and get the glasses and nibbles ready for aperitifs early in the day, then you can concentrate on the food. But don't be embarrassed to disappear into the kitchen occasionally for short periods—it shows that you are preparing freshly cooked food.

MENU PLANNING

Food should not go unnoticed—it should please the eye as well as the palate. The menus in this book have been planned to complement each other in style and content: light followed by fuller flavor, creaminess followed by sharpness and crunch, and so on. If you would prefer to mix and match the dishes, try and balance the flavors, textures and colors.

As rich desserts are becoming less popular, I have included a few savories —an old, Victorian idea regaining favor. Serve them after or instead of the dessert, followed by fruit, and cheese if you wish. They can also be served as snacks to go with drinks.

WINES AND DRINKS

Choosing a wine is personal and the suggestions are intended to be guides only. In some cases I have simply given one or two wines if the menu is more casual. Sometimes it is a nice idea to start with a dry sherry, or even drink a flower or herb tea throughout the meal.

Do be careful not to ply your guests with too much alcohol. Many will have to drive home, so it is a good idea to have bottles of mineral water as well.

NOTES

All spoon measurements are level.

Ovens should be preheated to the temperature specified.

Freshly ground black pepper is intended where pepper is listed.

Fresh herbs are used unless otherwise stated. If unobtainable, dried herbs can be substituted in cooked dishes but halve the quantities.

Use U.S. grade large eggs unless otherwise stated.

SEASONAL MENUS

This collection of four menus is based on the seasons, taking into account the availability of fresh foods and the type of meal that suits the weater—e.g. light in summer, warming in winter. Of course, with the wide range of imported ingredients and frozen foods now available, many of the dishes could be prepared all year round.

SPRING MENU FOR SIX
Sole and Asparagus Rolls, Celebration Roast Lamb, Tuiles Fruit Baskets.
Suggested Wines. *Appetizer:* Piesporter Michelsberg, or a Chablis. *Main Course:* Chianti Classico Riserva, or Beaujolais.

SUMMER MENU FOR FOUR
Watercress Stuffed Tomatoes, Salmon and Ginger Steaks, Summer Ramekins.
Suggested Wines. *Appetizer and Main Course:* A full-bodied white wine, such as white Burgundy.

AUTUMN MENU FOR FOUR
Zucchini and Chèvre Soufflés, Duck Breasts with Lemon Sauce, Fruit Shells.
Suggested Wines. *Appetizer:* A dry white wine. *Main Course:* A full-bodied red wine, such as Beaujolais.

WINTER MENU FOR SIX
Mussel and Saffron Soup, Spiced Beef with Almond Prunes, Georgian Silk.
Suggested Wines. *Appetizer:* Dry white wine. *Main Course:* A full red wine.

WATERCRESS STUFFED TOMATOES

4 large tomatoes
1 bunch watercress
1/2 cup cottage cheese
*   or soft goat's cheese*
2 scallions, chopped
*   finely*

1 teaspoon horseradish
*   cream or relish*
few curly endive leaves
1/2 cup vinaigrette dressing
salt and pepper to taste

Serves 4
Preparation time:
25 minutes
Freezing:
Not recommended

Illustrated below right: Zucchini and Chèvre Soufflés (page 10)

1. Cut the rounded ends off the tomatoes, scoop out the flesh and discard with the ends (or use for another dish).
2. Remove the stalks from half of the watercress and chop the leaves finely. Mix into the cheese with the scallions, horseradish, and salt and pepper. Pile into the tomato shells.
3. Place the remaining watercress and the curly endive in a bowl. Toss in half of the vinaigrette dressing.
4. Place the tomatoes on individual serving plates, trickle over the remaining vinaigrette dressing and garnish with the salad. Serve chilled.

SOLE AND ASPARAGUS ROLLS

*3 soles, skinned and
    filleted (bones and heads
    reserved)
1 cup dry white wine
1 onion, sliced
1 carrot, sliced
bouquet garni of bayleaf,
    parsley and thyme
2 cups water*

*12 asparagus spears
juice of ½ lemon
3 egg yolks
salt and pepper to taste
TO GARNISH:
¼ lb small mushrooms,
    cooked lightly in
    boiling water*

Serves 6
Preparation time:
45 minutes
Cooking time:
15–20 minutes
Freezing:
Not recommended

1. Place the fish bones and heads, wine, onion, carrot, bouquet garni, water, and salt and pepper in a pan and simmer for 20 minutes. Strain and reserve the stock.
2. Cut the asparagus about 4 inches from the tips. Place the stalks and reserved fish stock in a pan, cover and cook gently for 15 minutes, until quite soft; add the tips for the last 5 minutes. Drain, reserving the stock, and keep warm.
3. Season the fish with salt and pepper and sprinkle with the lemon juice. Fold the asparagus stalks in half, place on the fish and roll up. Place join side down in a shallow ovenproof dish.
4. Pour over the reserved stock, season with salt and pepper, cover and cook in a 375°F oven for 15–20 minutes, until tender. Transfer to a warmed serving dish with a slotted spoon and keep warm.
5. Strain 1¼ cups of the reserved stock into a saucepan and boil hard until reduced by half.
6. Place the egg yolks, and salt and pepper in a bowl over a pan of simmering water and whisk to a stiff foam. Stir in the reduced stock until creamy.
7. Spoon over the sole rolls and garnish with the asparagus tips and mushrooms to serve.

MUSSEL AND SAFFRON SOUP

*large pinch of saffron
    strands
8 lb mussels in shells
2½ cups fish stock or water
2 tablespoons butter
2 large onions, chopped*

*2 cloves garlic, crushed
⅔ cup dry white wine
¼ cup whole wheat flour
2½ cups milk
¼ cup chopped parsley
salt and pepper to taste*

1. Soak the saffron strands in 3 tablespoons boiling water for 15 minutes.
2. Discard any mussels that are open. Scrub the rest and place in a large saucepan. Add the stock or water, cover and simmer for about 5 minutes, until the shells open; discard any that do not open. Drain, reserving the liquor.
3. Scrape the mussels from the shells and set aside; reserve a few empty shells for garnishing.
4. Melt the butter in a pan, add the onion and garlic and fry gently for 3 minutes. Add the wine and cook, uncovered, until reduced by half.
5. Stir in the flour and cook for 2 minutes, then add the milk and reserved mussel liquor. Bring to the boil, stirring, then add the saffron and its soaking water. Season well with salt and pepper and simmer for 5 minutes.
6. Add the parsley and mussels and heat through gently; do not allow to boil or the mussels will toughen.
7. Replace a mussel in each of the reserved shells and float on the soup to serve.

Serves 6
Preparation time:
40 minutes
Cooking time:
15 minutes
Freezing:
Not recommended

ZUCCHINI AND CHÈVRE SOUFFLÉS

These individual soufflés can be prepared about an hour ahead and then cooked while your guests are having drinks, but they must be served straight from the oven.

2 tablespoons butter	*2 eggs, separated*
3 zucchini, chopped finely	*2 tablespoons freshly*
1 small onion, chopped	*grated Parmesan cheese*
1 clove garlic, crushed	*2 tablespoons dried*
1/3 cup all-purpose flour	*breadcrumbs*
2 oz soft goat's cheese,	*1 1/4 tablespoons slivered*
derinded and chopped	*almonds*
1/4 cup milk	*salt and pepper to taste*

Serves 4
Preparation time:
20 minutes
Cooking time:
About 25 minutes
Freezing:
Recommended at end of stage 4. Part thaw and cook for 30 minutes.

Illustrated on page 7

1. Melt the butter in a pan, add the zucchini, onion, garlic and 1 tablespoon water and saute gently for 5 minutes, until pulpy. Stir in the flour and simmer for 1 minute.
2. Add the cheese, milk, egg yolks, Parmesan, and salt and pepper, stirring well.
3. Whisk the egg whites until stiff, then fold in gently.
4. Lightly grease 4 individual soufflé dishes and coat with the breadcrumbs. Divide the mixture between the dishes and sprinkle with the almonds.
5. Bake in a 375°F oven for about 25 minutes, until well risen. Serve immediately.

CELEBRATION ROAST LAMB

If serving a crown roast, fill the center with a selection of crisp vegetables to serve.

large crown roast or leg of	*bouquet garni of bayleaf,*
lamb, weighing 5 lb	*thyme and parsley*
2 cloves garlic, sliced	*2 tablespoons cornstarch,*
2 rosemary sprigs	*blended with 1*
2 1/2 cups lamb stock	*tablespoon water*
1 tablespoon salad oil	*1/4 cup ginger wine*
1 onion, chopped	*2 tablespoons redcurrant*
1 carrot, chopped	*jelly*
1/3 cup red wine vinegar	*rosemary sprigs to garnish*

1. Stab the lamb in several places with a sharp pointed knife and place the garlic and rosemary in each cut. Weigh

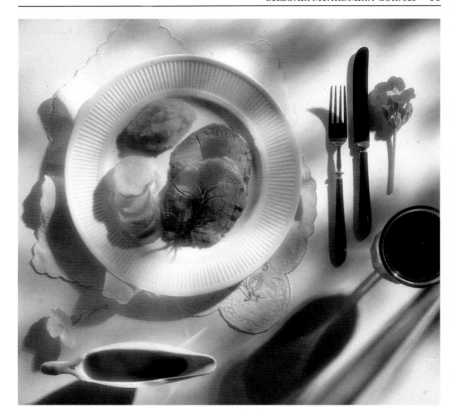

the joint, allowing 20–25 minutes per lb, depending on how well done you like your meat, and cook in a 350°F oven for the calculated time. Place the lamb on a serving dish and keep warm. Drain off the fat from the pan.

2. Pour the stock into the pan and scrape up all the meaty residue. Reserve.

3. Heat the oil in a pan, add the onion and carrot and saute for 10 minutes. Add the vinegar and boil until it evaporates.

4. Add the reserved stock and bouquet garni and simmer for 5 minutes. Stir in the blended cornstarch, then add the ginger wine and redcurrant jelly and simmer for 3 minutes. Strain into a sauce boat.

5. Garnish the lamb with rosemary sprigs and serve with Potatoes Boulangère (page 77), a vegetable puree, such as carrot (see page 79) and a green vegetable. Hand the sauce separately.

Serves 6
Preparation time:
15 minutes
Cooking time:
1½–2 hours
Freezing:
Not recommended

DUCK BREASTS WITH LEMON SAUCE

*4 duck breasts, each
  weighing ⅓ lb, skinned
whole wheat flour for
  coating
1 tablespoon olive oil
1 tablespoon butter*

*1 large clove garlic, sliced
juice of 1 lemon
2 teaspoons sugar
salt and pepper to taste
lemon twists to garnish*

**Serves 4
Preparation time:**
10 minutes
Cooking time:
10–15 minutes
Freezing:
Not recommended

1. Toss the duck breasts in flour to coat evenly.
2. Heat the oil and butter gently in a pan, add the garlic and fry slowly until it starts to brown; discard.
3. Increase the heat and add the duck breasts. Fry for about 5 minutes on each side or until cooked to your liking.
4. Pour in the lemon juice, sprinkle with the sugar and season with salt and pepper.
5. Slice the breasts diagonally and garnish with twists of lemon. Serve with Baby Rösti (page 78) and Peas with Lettuce (page 76).

SALMON AND GINGER STEAKS

*4 salmon steaks, each
  weighing ½ lb
¼ cup butter, softened
2 teaspoons grated fresh
  root ginger
3 oz fennel, sliced thinly*

*2 carrots and ½ leek, cut
  into julienne strips
2–3 tablespoons dry sherry
  (optional)
salt and pepper to taste*

**Serves 4
Preparation time:**
15 minutes
Cooking time:
20–25 minutes
Freezing:
Not recommended

1. Place the salmon steaks in a shallow ovenproof dish and season with salt and pepper.
2. Mix the butter with the ginger and spread half on the salmon steaks.
3. Blanch the vegetables in boiling water for 2 minutes. Drain and place on the salmon.
4. Sprinkle with the sherry, if using, and top with the remaining butter. Season lightly with salt and pepper.
5. Cover and cook in a 375°F oven for 20–25 minutes or until cooked.
6. Serve with small thin-skinned potatoes, Green Beans in Tomato Concasse (page 76) and a crisp salad.

SPICED BEEF WITH ALMOND PRUNES

6 slices braising beef, each
weighing 1/3 lb and
about 3/4 inch thick
2 onions, sliced
2 carrots, sliced
2 cloves garlic, crushed
1 teaspoon ground
coriander
1/2 teaspoon ground cloves
1 1/4 cups red wine
3 tablespoons brandy
(optional)
2 tablespoons olive oil
1 cup diced bacon

2 tablespoons whole wheat
flour
2 cups strong beef stock
large bouquet garni of
bayleaf, parsley and
thyme
3 thin strips orange rind
12 large pitted prunes
12 whole almonds
salt and pepper to taste
FOR THE FLEURONS:
1/2 × 8 oz package puff
pastry
beaten egg to glaze

Serves 6
Preparation time:
25 minutes, plus
marinating
Cooking time:
2 1/4 hours
Freezing:
Recommended

1. Place the beef, onions, carrots, garlic and spices in a large dish, pour over the wine and brandy, if using, and leave to marinate overnight.
2. Drain, reserving the marinade.
3. Heat the oil in a pan, add the beef and fry quickly on both sides to brown. Remove and set aside.
4. Add the marinated vegetables and the bacon to the pan and saute for about 5 minutes.
5. Add the flour and cook, stirring, for 2 minutes. Add the reserved marinade and the stock, bring to the boil and cook for 2 minutes.
6. Transfer to a casserole and add the meat, herbs, orange rind, and salt and pepper. Cover and cook in a 325°F oven for about 2 hours or until tender.
7. Stuff the prunes with the almonds and add to the casserole for the last 20 minutes of cooking.
8. To make the fleurons, roll out the pastry thinly. Using a fluted 2 inch cutter, stamp out half moon shapes. Brush with beaten egg. Increase the oven temperature to 400°F and bake for 10–15 minutes, until golden. Scatter on top of the casserole.
9. Serve with baked potatoes, Creamed Sprouts (page 77) and crisply cooked seasonal vegetables.

SUMMER RAMEKINS

1 passion fruit
1 lb mixed soft fruit, e.g.
   strawberries, raspberries,
   cherries
¼ cup honey
2 tablespoons water

8 small slices whole wheat
   bread
TO SERVE:
1–2 tablespoons whipping
   cream
mint leaves to decorate

Serves 4
Preparation time:
20 minutes, plus
chilling
Cooking time:
5 minutes
Freezing:
Recommended

1. Cut the passion fruit in half and scoop out the pulp.
2. Place the passion fruit pulp and prepared soft fruit in a pan, add the honey and water and cook for about 5 minutes, until the juice runs. Leave to cool.
3. Lightly grease 4 individual ramekins and line the bases with foil or waxed paper.
4. Cut out 8 rounds of bread the size of the ramekins and put one in each dish.
5. Spoon on the fruit, draining slightly; reserve ⅔ cup juice. Rub this through a sieve and set aside.
6. Top the fruit in the ramekins with the remaining bread, weigh down lightly with cups and chill overnight.
7. Turn out onto individual plates and spoon over the reserved juice, thinned with a little water if necessary.
8. Dip a skewer into the cream, then swirl into the sauce around each pudding. Decorate with mint to serve.

TUILES FRUIT BASKETS

The tuiles can be made in advance and stored in an airtight container. Prepare the fruit sauces ahead, but spoon in the prepared fruits just before serving.

FOR THE TUILES:
3 egg whites
½ cup superfine sugar
¾ cup sifted all-purpose
   flour
2 tablespoons butter,
   melted
grated rind of 1 orange
FOR THE GOOSEBERRY
   AND KIWI SAUCE:
1 lb gooseberries
a few elderflowers
   (optional)
¼ cup honey

2 kiwi fruit, peeled
½ cup curd cheese or
   farmer's cheese
FOR THE RASPBERRY
   COULIS:
1 cup raspberries
2 tablespoons powdered
   sugar
TO SERVE:
1 lb mixed soft fruit, e.g.
   strawberries, raspberries,
   peaches, plums, apricots
powdered sugar for
   sprinkling

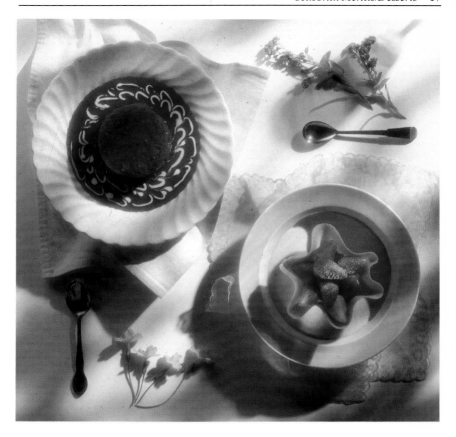

1. Beat the ingredients for the tuiles together until smooth.

2. Place heaped teaspoons of the mixture well apart on well greased baking sheets, 2 per sheet, and bake in a 350°F oven for 10 minutes.

3. Scoop off immediately with a palette knife and place over an orange or upturned cup. Press down lightly to mold, then place on a rack to cool.

4. Place the gooseberries, elderflowers, if using, and honey in a pan and cook for about 10 minutes, until pulpy. Discard the elderflowers, if used.

5. Cool slightly, then place in a blender or food processor with the kiwi fruit and cheese and work until smooth. Rub through a sieve.

6. Puree the raspberries and powdered sugar in a blender or food processor, then rub through a sieve. Chill both sauces until required.

7. Fill the tuiles with fruit, dust with powdered sugar and serve on a pool of the two sauces on individual plates.

Serves 6 (but the mixture makes extra baskets)
Preparation time: 30 minutes
Cooking time: 30 minutes
Freezing: Not recommended

FRAGRANT FRUIT SHELLS

1 pineapple, halved
1 papaya or mango,
  peeled and sliced
1 kiwi fruit, peeled, halved
  and sliced

2 teaspoons orange flower
  water
2 cups sliced strawberries
1 tablespoon powdered
  sugar

Serves 4
Preparation time:
15 minutes
Freezing:
Not recommended

1. Cut the pineapple flesh from the shells, leaving the shells intact.
2. Mix the pineapple, papaya or mango, kiwi fruit and orange flower water together with a third of the strawberries. Pile back into the pineapple shells.
3. Puree the remaining strawberries with the powdered sugar in a blender or food processor.
4. Trickle a little of the strawberry puree over the fruit. Serve the remainder separately.

GEORGIAN SILK

²/₃ cup freshly squeezed
  lemon juice, strained
  (juice of about 4
  lemons)
3 tablespoons medium
  sherry
4 strips lemon rind
3 tablespoons sugar
1 envelope gelatin

1³/₄ cups freshly squeezed
  orange juice, strained
  (juice of about 4 large
  oranges)
4 strips orange rind
¹/₃ cup whipping cream
  (optional)
mint leaves to decorate

Serves 6
Preparation time:
20 minutes, plus
setting time
Cooking time:
6 minutes
Freezing:
Not recommended

1. Make the lemon juice and sherry up to 2½ cups with boiling water. Place in a pan, add the lemon rind and sugar, then simmer for 3 minutes. Remove from the heat.
2. Sprinkle in half of the gelatin, stirring briskly until dissolved. Leave to cool.
3. Strain into 6 wine glasses and chill until set; about 4 hours.
4. Place the orange juice and rind in a pan, bring to the boil, then simmer for 3 minutes. Add sugar to taste, if required. Sprinkle in the remaining gelatin, stirring until dissolved. Leave to cool, then strain.
5. When the lemon layer has set, pour over the orange gelatin and leave to set.
6. If wished, pour 1 tablespoon cream over each serving. Decorate with mint and serve accompanied by dessert biscuits.

ANYTIME MENUS

MENU FOR SIX

Leek, Tomato and Cheese Salad, Ella's Roast Pork, Choux Buns with Mango Cream

Suggested wines. *Appetizer:* Chilled dry sherry if you wish. *Main course:* Rosé or Californian Zinfandel.

MENU FOR FOUR

Pasta with Tomato Sauce and Zucchini, Haddock and Whiting Turban, Coffee and Walnut Roulade.

Suggested wines. *Appetizer:* Light red wine. *Main course:* Burgundy, Chardonnay.

MENU FOR FOUR

Avocado with Two Caviars, Lamb with Watercress in Filo, Apples with Sauternes Sauce

Suggested wines. *Appetizer:* Light white wine. *Main course:* Any Beaujolais.

MENU FOR FOUR

Warm Spinach Salad, Guinea Hen with Cucumber, Brandied Bread Pudding.

Suggested wines. *Appetizer:* Crisp, dry white wine. *Main course:* A full-flavored, robust red wine.

MENU FOR FOUR

Caesar Salad, Pork Dijonnaise, Apricot Amaretti Fool.

Suggested wine. *Main Course:* Smooth, full-flavored red wine.

AVOCADO WITH TWO CAVIARS

2 large ripe avocados, peeled, halved and pitted
FOR THE DRESSING:
2/3 cup sour cream
1 tablespoon wine vinegar
2 tablespoons sunflower oil
1/2 teaspoon dry mustard

1 teaspoon superfine sugar
salt and pepper to taste
TO SERVE:
2 tablespoons each red and black lumpfish roe caviar
snipped chives (optional)

Serves 4
Preparation time:
10 minutes
Freezing:
Not recommended

1. Slash the avocado halves from the wide base almost to the top and fan out on 4 serving plates.
2. Whisk the dressing ingredients together. Pour some around the avocados; serve the rest separately.
3. Garnish with alternate mounds of caviar and sprinkle the dressing with chives if you wish. Serve immediately.

CAESAR SALAD

In America in the 1920s, one Caesar Cardini devised a salad based on simple ingredients—bread, lettuce, Parmesan cheese, eggs and the best olive oil. It became very popular with the Hollywood movie world and is now a culinary legend.

3 cloves garlic
⅓ cup virgin olive oil
4 slices whole wheat bread, crusts removed, diced
1 romaine lettuce
⅔ cup grated Parmesan cheese

FOR THE DRESSING:
2 teaspoons French mustard
1 teaspoon Worcestershire sauce
2 tablespoons freshly squeezed lemon juice
1 egg, beaten
salt and pepper to taste

Serves 4
Preparation time:
15 minutes
Cooking time:
10 minutes
Freezing:
Not recommended

1. Rub the inside of 4 small salad bowls with one of the cloves of garlic.
2. Chop the others and slowly heat in 3 tablespoons of the oil for about 5 minutes; do not allow it to burn. Discard.
3. Toss the bread in the oil, spread on a baking sheet and bake in a 375°F oven for 10 minutes, until crisp. Leave to cool.
4. Whisk the dressing ingredients together with the remaining oil.
5. Place the lettuce in the bowls, sprinkle over the cheese and pour in the dressing. Toss well, sprinkle with the croutons and serve immediately.

PASTA WITH TOMATO SAUCE AND ZUCCHINI

½ lb fresh fettuccine or ⅓ lb dried spaghetti
2 tablespoons butter
2 cloves garlic, crushed
2 tablespoons olive oil
⅓ lb zucchini, cut into thin sticks
⅔ cup grated Parmesan cheese (optional)

FOR THE SAUCE:
1 tablespoon olive oil
1 onion, chopped
4 medium-size tomatoes, skinned, seeded and sliced
1¼ cups tomato juice
2 tablespoons dry vermouth
salt and pepper to taste

1. First prepare the sauce. Heat the oil in a pan, add the onion and saute for 5 minutes. Add the remaining ingredients, cover and simmer for 15 minutes. Keep warm.

2. Cook the pasta according to package instructions. Drain, rinse and toss in half of the butter and 1 clove garlic. Keep warm.

3. Just before serving, heat the remaining butter and the olive oil in a pan, add the remaining garlic and the zucchini and stir-fry for about 3 minutes, until just tender.

4. Serve the pasta with the sauce, topped with the zucchini. Sprinkle with Parmesan, if you wish.

Serves 4
Preparation time: 15 minutes
Cooking time: 20–25 minutes
Freezing: Recommended for sauce only

LEEK, TOMATO AND CHEESE SALAD

6 leeks, sliced
1 1/4 cups light stock
6 large tomatoes, skinned,
  seeded and sliced
8 oz Mozzarella cheese,
  sliced
FOR THE DRESSING:
1/4 cup olive or sunflower
  oil
2 tablespoons freshly
  squeezed orange juice

2 tablespoons wine
  vinegar
1 teaspoon coarse-grain
  mustard
1 teaspoon honey
3 tablespoons chopped
  parsley
1 tablespoon chopped basil
salt and pepper to taste

Serves 6
Preparation time:
15 minutes, plus
chilling
Cooking time:
2 minutes
Freezing:
Not recommended

1. Blanch the leeks in the boiling stock for 2 minutes. Drain, place in a bowl and season with salt and pepper.
2. Mix the dressing ingredients together and toss into the leeks while still warm. Leave to cool, then add the tomatoes. Mix together lightly, then chill until required.
3. Transfer to individual plates, arrange the cheese on top and season lightly with salt and pepper.

WARM SPINACH SALAD

If quails' eggs are unobtainable, use 3 chopped hens' eggs.

1 lb young spinach leaves
1 large head Belgium
  endive
1 clove garlic, halved
1/3 lb mushrooms, sliced
12 quails' eggs,
  hard-boiled and halved
FOR THE DRESSING:
2 tablespoons olive oil

1 teaspoon sesame oil
  (optional)
1 cup diced bacon
2 tablespoons fruit wine
  vinegar
1 teaspoon coarse-grain
  mustard
salt and pepper to taste

Serves 4
Preparation time:
25 minutes
Cooking time:
8 minutes
Freezing:
Not recommended

1. Tear or shred the spinach and Belgium endive leaves.
2. Rub the inside of 4 individual salad bowls or plates with the garlic; discard. Arrange the spinach and Belgium endive in the bowls or plates. Add the mushrooms and eggs.
3. Heat the oil(s) in a pan, add the bacon and fry until crisp. Remove with a slotted spoon; sprinkle on the salad.
4. Add the vinegar, mustard, and salt and pepper to the pan and allow to bubble. Serve hot, separately, for guests to toss on their salad themselves.

HADDOCK AND WHITING TURBAN

This can be prepared in advance—completely ready, just to pop in the oven. Do not cook in advance or the spinach will lose its bright green color as it stands.

6–8 large spinach or
lettuce leaves
1 lb whiting fillets, skinned
and halved lengthways
1 1/2 lb smoked haddock
fillets, skinned
2 egg whites
1 teaspoon mild curry
powder
1 teaspoon turmeric

1 teaspoon salt
3/4 cup whipping cream
pepper to taste
FOR THE SAUCE:
2/3 cup sour cream
2 egg yolks
1/2 teaspoon Dijon
mustard
juice of 1/2 lemon

Serves 4
Preparation time:
25 minutes, plus
chilling
Cooking time:
30 minutes
Freezing:
Not recommended

1. Blanch the spinach or lettuce in boiling water for 30 seconds, or until just limp; drain well.
2. Arrange about 6 whiting fillets, skinned side inwards, alternately with the spinach or lettuce, around the edge of a greased 8 inch ring mold, leaving a few gaps.
3. Place the haddock, remaining whiting, egg whites, curry, turmeric, salt and pepper in a blender or food processor and work until smooth.
4. Chill for 1 hour, then process again, gradually adding the cream.
5. Press the mixture carefully but firmly into the prepared mold. Fold over any spinach or whiting ends. Cover with greased foil.
6. Place in a roasting pan half-filled with water and cook in a 350°F oven for 30 minutes. Drain off the juices and reserve for the sauce. Turn out the Turban onto a serving plate.
7. To make the sauce, place all the ingredients, with the reserved juices and salt and pepper to taste, in a blender or food processor and work until smooth. Heat gently.
8. Serve the Turban hot or cold, with thin-skinned potatoes and snow peas. Serve the sauce separately.

GUINEA HEN WITH CUCUMBER

2 tablespoons salad oil	*⅓ cucumber, peeled, sliced*
1 guinea hen, jointed into	*and seeded*
4 portions	*3 tablespoons whipping*
⅔ cup rosé wine	*cream*
1 thyme sprig	*1 teaspoon grenadine*
1¼ cups light stock	*(optional)*
6 scallions, sliced	*salt and pepper to taste*

1. Heat the oil in a pan, add the guinea hen portions and fry until browned. Drain off the oil, then pour in the wine. Add the thyme, and salt and pepper, cover and cook for 15 minutes, turning once. Transfer the guinea hen to a warmed serving dish and keep warm.

2. Add the stock, scallions and cucumber to the pan and cook, uncovered, for 5 minutes. Remove the vegetables with a slotted spoon and arrange on the serving dish.

3. Boil the liquid left in the pan until reduced to about 1¼ cups. Stir in the cream and grenadine, if using. Pour over the guinea hen. Serve with Peas with Lettuce (page 76) and thin-skinned potatoes.

Serves 4
Preparation time:
15 minutes
Cooking time:
About 35 minutes
Freezing:
Not recommended

ELLA'S ROAST PORK

This is a popular dish of a Portuguese friend of mine. It looks best made with a long rolled joint of pork.

*3 lb rolled loin or leg of
pork, or smoked loin of
pork
2½ cups thinly sliced
carrots
½ cup raisins
1¼ cups light stock
⅔ cup port
2 tablespoons all-purpose
flour, blended with 1
tablespoon water
(optional)*

*FOR THE MARINADE:
3 tablespoons sunflower
oil
1½ tablespoons soy sauce
juice of 1 lemon
1 tablespoon wine vinegar
1 clove garlic, crushed
salt and pepper to taste
TO GARNISH:
⅓ cup pine nuts, toasted*

**Serves 6
Preparation time:**
25 minutes, plus
marinating
Cooking time:
About 1½ hours
Freezing:
Recommended

1. Mix the marinade ingredients together and place in a large, strong plastic bag. Add the pork, carrots and raisins and leave overnight.
2. Lift out the pork. Remove the carrots and raisins with a slotted spoon and arrange in a line, in a roasting pan. Put the pork on top. Pour in the stock and marinade.
3. Roast in a 325°F oven for about 1½ hours or until tender, basting frequently and topping up with boiling water as necessary.
4. Spoon the carrots and raisins onto a warmed serving platter. Slice the pork and arrange on top.
5. Pour the port into the pan juices and allow to bubble for 2 minutes; if you wish, thicken with the blended flour. Check the seasoning. Pour a little of the sauce over the meat and strain the rest into a jug.
6. Garnish with the pine nuts and serve with Brown Rice with Broccoli, Celery and Nuts (page 78) and spinach.

LAMB WITH WATERCRESS IN FILO

*⅓ cup butter
1 small onion, chopped
1 clove garlic, crushed
1 bunch watercress,
chopped
2 tablespoons wine
2 lb boned leg of lamb
1 tablespoon salad oil*

*1 teaspoon chopped
rosemary leaves
2 oz Feta cheese, sliced
thinly (optional)
4 sheets filo pastry
salt and pepper to taste
rosemary sprigs to garnish*

1. Melt a third of the butter in a pan, add the onion and garlic and saute for 3 minutes. Add the watercress and wine, cover and simmer for 3 minutes. Puree in a blender or food processor and leave to cool.

2. Trim the lamb of all fat and sinews, then cut into 4 long fillets.

3. Heat the oil in a pan, add the lamb, rosemary, and salt and pepper, and fry for 3 minutes on each side. Drain on paper towels and leave to cool.

4. Slash the fillets in 4 places, almost through. Fill each slash with cheese, if using, and watercress puree. Spread the remaining puree on top. Season with salt and pepper.

5. Melt the remaining butter and use half to brush the filo sheets. Fold in half, place a fillet on each and wrap up like an envelope. Glaze with the remaining butter.

6. Place on a baking sheet and bake in a 375°F oven for 25 minutes. Serve hot with a green salad and cherry tomatoes. Garnish with rosemary.

Serves 4
Preparation time: 15 minutes, plus cooling time
Cooking time: 25 minutes
Freezing: Not recommended

PORK DIJONNAISE

2 tablespoons sunflower oil	*1/4 lb mushrooms, sliced*
4 large pork loin chops	*3 thyme or tarragon sprigs*
1/2 lb pearl onions	*3 tablespoons coarse-grain mustard*
2 cloves garlic, crushed	*2/3 cup sour cream*
1/4 lb sliced bacon	*salt and pepper to taste*
1 1/4 cups apple cider	*thyme sprigs to garnish*

Serves 4
Preparation time:
15 minutes
Cooking time:
About 25 minutes
Freezing:
Recommended

1. Heat the oil in a pan, add the chops and cook for 2 minutes on each side. Remove and set aside.
2. Add the onions, garlic and bacon to the pan and saute for about 3 minutes.
3. Add the cider and boil for 3 minutes, or until reduced by a third. Add the mushrooms, herbs, mustard, and salt and pepper, stir, then cook for 2 minutes.
4. Return the chops to the pan, spoon over the sauce, cover and simmer for about 12 minutes, until tender.
5. Transfer the chops to a warmed serving platter. Stir the cream into the sauce in the pan and reheat gently; do not allow to boil.
6. Spoon the sauce over the chops and garnish with thyme. Serve with noodles, Carrots Sweet and Sour (page 77) and a green vegetable.

APRICOT AMARETTI FOOL

1 1/2 cups dried apricots, soaked	*3 cups crushed amaretti biscuits*
1/4 cup honey	*3 tablespoons brandy*
1 1/2 cups Greek strained yogurt	*3 egg whites*

Serves 4
Preparation time:
10 minutes, plus
soaking time and
chilling
Cooking time:
5 minutes
Freezing:
Not recommended

1. Place the apricots, honey and 2–3 tablespoons of water in a pan and cook for 5 minutes. Leave to cool, then puree in a blender or food processor.
2. Stir in three quarters of the yogurt and biscuits, and the brandy.
3. Whisk the egg whites until stiff, then fold in. Chill until required.
4. Top with the remaining yogurt and sprinkle with the remaining cookie crumbs to serve.

CHOUX BUNS WITH MANGO CREAM

These choux buns are made with half the usual amount of fat, which makes them light and crisp. Fill just before serving to keep them crisp.

3 tablespoons butter
¾ cup plus 2 tablespoons
*   water*
1 cup all-purpose flour
3 eggs, beaten
few slivered almonds
FOR THE FILLING:
2 ripe mangos, peeled

few drops orange flower
*   water (optional)*
1 ripe banana, mashed
1¼ cups whipping cream,
*   whipped*
TO SERVE:
powdered sugar to dust
1 kiwi fruit, sliced

Serves 6
Preparation time:
25 minutes
Cooking time:
About 30 minutes
Freezing:
Recommended for
buns only

1. Place the butter and water in a pan and heat gently until melted, then bring to the boil. Add the flour all at once and beat well until the dough leaves the side of the pan. Leave to cool for 10 minutes.
2. Gradually beat in all but 2 tablespoons of the egg, to form a stiff dropping consistency.
3. Drop into 6 mounds on a greased baking sheet, spacing them well apart. Glaze with the remaining egg and sprinkle with the almonds. Bake in a 400°F oven for about 30 minutes, until crisp and golden.
4. Split in half, scrape out any uncooked dough and return to the oven for 2 minutes to crisp. Cool on a rack while preparing the filling.
5. Slice one mango and set aside. Puree the other mango, with the orange flower water if using, in a blender or food processor.
6. Mix the banana and cream together and spoon into the bun bases. Trickle over the mango puree, cover with the bun tops and dust with powdered sugar.
7. Serve with the sliced mango and kiwi fruit.

APPLES WITH SAUTERNES SAUCE

4 cooking apples, cored
2 tablespoons marmalade
½ cup raisins or golden
*   raisins*

⅓ cup light brown sugar,
*   packed*
⅔ cup Sauternes wine
1 orange

1. Score the apples round the middle. Place in a shallow ovenproof dish. Mix the marmalade and fruit together and use to fill each cavity.

2. Sprinkle the sugar around, then pour in the wine. Cook in a 375°F oven for 1 hour, basting occasionally.
3. Meanwhile, pare the rind from the orange and cut into shreds. Squeeze the juice and heat gently in a pan.
4. Transfer the apples to a serving dish. Drain off the juices from the cooking dish and stir into the hot orange juice.
5. Decorate the apples with the orange strips and serve with the orange sauce, and cream or yogurt if you wish.

Serves 4
Preparation time:
10 minutes
Cooking time:
1 hour
Freezing:
Recommended

COFFEE AND WALNUT ROULADE

4 eggs, separated
1/2 cup superfine sugar
1 tablespoon instant coffee
  powder
3/4 cup ground walnuts
superfine sugar for
  sprinkling
walnut halves to decorate

FOR THE FILLING:
1 tablespoon instant coffee
  powder
1 tablespoon hot water
2/3 cup heavy cream,
  whipped
2 tablespoons superfine
  sugar
1 egg white
1 tablespoon whisky

Serves 4
Preparation time:
20 minutes
Cooking time:
20 minutes
Freezing:
Recommended

1. Line a 9 × 12 inch jelly roll pan with foil and grease lightly.
2. Whisk the egg yolks, sugar and coffee powder together in a bowl over a pan of gently simmering water until thick and creamy. Leave to cool, whisking occasionally.
3. Whisk the egg whites until stiff, then fold gently into the coffee mixture with the ground walnuts.
4. Spoon into the prepared pan and bake in a 350°F oven for 20 minutes.
5. Turn out onto a sheet of waxed paper sprinkled with superfine sugar. Carefully peel off the foil and roll up in the paper. Leave to cool while making the filling.
6. Dissolve the coffee in the water. Leave to cool, then whisk into the cream with the sugar.
7. Whisk the egg white until stiff, then fold into the coffee cream with the whisky.
8. Carefully unroll the roulade, remove the paper and spread with most of the filling. Re-roll and decorate with the remaining cream and the walnut halves.

BRANDIED BREAD PUDDING

A sophisticated version of a traditional pudding. A light sauce separates out from the pudding when it is cooked, so cream to serve is unnecessary.

2/3 cup raisins
grated rind and juice of
  1 orange
1/4 cup brandy
9 slices whole wheat bread,
  crusts removed, buttered
  and halved diagonally

2 1/2 cups milk
1/4 cup light brown sugar,
  packed
2 eggs, plus 1 yolk
grated nutmeg for
  sprinkling

1. Place the raisins and orange juice in a pan and heat gently for about 2 minutes. Add half of the brandy. Cool for 1 hour.

2. Arrange alternate layers of bread and raisins in a 1½ quart ovenproof dish. Sprinkle with the remaining brandy.

3. Place the milk, sugar and orange rind in a pan and heat gently.

4. Beat the eggs and yolk in a large bowl, then whisk in the hot milk. Gradually pour over the bread, allowing it to soak in. Set aside for 1 hour or overnight.

5. Sprinkle with nutmeg, place in a roasting pan half-filled with boiling water and cook in a 375°F oven for 1 hour, until risen and crunchy on top. Serve hot.

Serves 4
Preparation time:
15 minutes, plus cooling and standing time
Cooking time:
1 hour
Freezing:
Not recommended

VEGETARIAN MENUS

MENU FOR FOUR
Artichokes with Avocado Cream, Spinach and Lentil Galette, Brown Bread Ice Cream.
Suggested wines. *Appetizer:* Verduzzo Del Piave. *Main course:* Corbières or Crozes-Hermitage.

MENU FOR FOUR
Mushroom Croustades, Eggplant Parmigiana, Bananas with Orange and Rum.
Suggested wines. *Appetizer:* Amontillado sherry. *Main course:* Chianti Classico.

MENU FOR FOUR
Bean and Cashew Nut Salad, Malfatti with Red Pepper Sauce, Soft Fruit Compote with Liqueur Cream.
Suggested wine. A light Italian-style red or white.

MENU FOR FOUR
Four Fruit Vinaigrette Salad, Zucchini and Rice Streudels, Raspberry and Nut Meringue.
Suggested wine. *Main course:* Dry red or white wine.

ARTICHOKES WITH AVOCADO CREAM

To eat an artichoke, work from the outside in, pulling off the leaves and dipping the fleshy base into the sauce. Eat the fleshy part, then discard the leaves. Eat the heart with a knife and fork. Do not prepare the avocado cream more than 30 minutes in advance.

4 globe artichokes
juice of 1 lemon
1 large avocado, peeled, halved and pitted
3 tablespoons sour cream or plain yogurt

3 tablespoons mayonnaise
2 scallions, chopped
1 teaspoon Worcestershire sauce
salt and pepper to taste
chopped parsley to serve

Serves 4
Preparation time: 20 minutes, plus chilling
Cooking time: 40–50 minutes
Freezing: Not recommended

1. Remove the stalk from the artichokes and trim the leaf tops if you wish. Boil in plenty of salted water, with half of the lemon juice added, for 40–50 minutes, until the base leaves pull off easily. Drain upside down, cool and chill.
2. Part the leaves and remove the center hairy choke with a teaspoon.
3. Blend the remaining ingredients together to make a smooth cream. Spoon into the center of each artichoke and sprinkle with parsley to serve.

MUSHROOM CROUSTADES

1 small uncut loaf
¼ cup butter
2 tablespoons salad oil
3 tablespoons vegetable
* stock or water*
¾ lb mushrooms, sliced
1 tablespoon all-purpose
* flour*

¾ cup plus 2 tablespoons
* milk*
2 tablespoons chopped
* parsley*
1 thyme sprig, chopped
salt and pepper to taste
thyme sprigs to garnish

Serves 4
Preparation time:
20 minutes
Cooking time:
About 30 minutes
Freezing:
Recommended for
cases only

1. Cut off a thin slice from each end of the loaf and discard. Trim off the crusts and cut the bread into 4 rectangles 1¼ inch thick, measuring 3½ × 2 inches. Hollow out the center of each piece, leaving a shell about ½ inch thick.
2. Melt 3 tablespoons of the butter with the oil and lightly brush the top of the cases. Place on a baking sheet, buttered side up, and bake in a 325°F oven for about 30 minutes, until crisp and golden. Drain on paper towels.
3. Meanwhile, melt the remaining butter in a pan, add the stock or water, mushrooms and flour, cover, shake well and simmer for 5 minutes. Stir in the milk, herbs, and salt and pepper and simmer for 1 minute.
4. Divide between the croustades and serve immediately, garnished with thyme.

FOUR-FRUIT VINAIGRETTE SALAD

1 ripe papaya, peeled,
* seeded and cut into*
* chunks*
1 large pear, peeled, cored
* and cut into chunks*
2 large grapefruit, peeled
* and cut into segments*

½ honeydew melon,
* peeled, seeded and cut*
* into chunks*
⅓ cup vinaigrette dressing
1 tablespoon chopped mint
mint sprigs to garnish

Serves 4
Preparation time:
20 minutes, plus
chilling
Freezing:
Not recommended

1. Mix the fruits together in a bowl. Pour over the dressing, sprinkle with the mint and toss well.
2. Transfer to sundae or small glass dishes and chill until required. Garnish with mint to serve.

VARIATION
Slice the fruits and arrange on individual serving plates. Mix the dressing and mint together and trickle over the fruits. Chill and garnish with mint to serve.

BEAN AND CASHEW NUT SALAD

*2/3 cup dried navy beans,
  soaked overnight*
*1/2 small fennel or 2 celery
  sticks, sliced thinly*
*1 red dessert apple, cored
  and cut into chunks*
3 scallions, sliced
*1/3 cup roasted salted
  cashew nuts*
FOR THE DRESSING:
1/4 cup sunflower oil

juice of 1 lemon
1 tablespoon wine vinegar
1 tablespoon sweet sherry
1/2 teaspoon dried thyme
*1 teaspoon coarse-grain
  mustard*
salt and pepper to taste
TO SERVE:
*4 large radicchio or
  romaine lettuce leaves*

Serves 4
Preparation time:
15 minutes, plus
soaking time
Cooking time:
About 1 hour
Freezing:
Recommended for
beans only

1. Drain the beans, place in a pan and cover with cold water. Bring to the boil and boil rapidly for 10 minutes, then simmer for about 50 minutes or until tender; drain.
2. Place the dressing ingredients in a screw-top jar, shake well to blend, then pour over the warm beans in a bowl.
3. When cold, mix with the remaining salad ingredients.
4. Arrange the radicchio or lettuce leaves on individual serving plates and top with the salad to serve.

MALFATTI WITH RED PEPPER SAUCE

Malfatti are light Italian spinach dumplings.

1 lb spinach
1 onion, chopped finely
1 clove garlic, crushed
1 tablespoon olive oil
1 1/2 cups Ricotta cheese
3 eggs, beaten
1 cup dried breadcrumbs
1/2 cup whole wheat flour
1 teaspoon salt
*2/3 cup grated Parmesan
  cheese*

grated nutmeg to taste
*2 tablespoons butter,
  melted*
FOR THE SAUCE:
2 red peppers
2 tablespoons salad oil
1 onion, chopped
*14 oz can chopped
  tomatoes*
2/3 cup water
salt and pepper to taste

1. First prepare the sauce. Broil the peppers until the skins blacken and blister. Leave to cool, then remove the skin and seeds. Chop the flesh.
2. Heat the oil in a pan, add the onion and peppers and saute for 5 minutes. Add the tomatoes, water, and salt and pepper, cover and simmer for 15 minutes. Puree in a

blender or food processor, then rub through a sieve. Keep warm.

3. Remove any large stalks from the spinach, then blanch the leaves in boiling water for 1 minute. Drain well, squeeze dry, then chop finely.

4. Mix with the onion, garlic, oil, Ricotta cheese, eggs, breadcrumbs, flour, salt, half of the Parmesan, and pepper and nutmeg. Roll into 24 small 'logs' with wet hands, or shape into 12–16 ovals (quenelles) using 2 spoons.

5. Drop in batches into gently boiling salted water and cook for 5 minutes. Remove, drain and toss in the butter.

6. Arrange on individual plates, on a pool of the sauce. Sprinkle with the remaining Parmesan to serve.

Serves 4
Preparation time:
30 minutes
Cooking time:
30 minutes
Freezing:
Not recommended

SPINACH AND LENTIL GALETTE

FOR THE PANCAKES:
1/2 cup whole wheat or
    buckwheat flour
1/2 cup all-purpose flour
pinch of salt
2 eggs
1 1/4 cups milk
FOR THE 1ST FILLING:
1 fennel, sliced thinly
1 onion, chopped
3/4 cup red lentils
3 tomatoes, skinned and
    chopped
2 cups vegetable stock

1 tablespoon chopped
    marjoram
FOR THE 2ND FILLING:
2 tablespoons butter
1 lb spinach, shredded
1 onion, chopped
1 clove garlic, crushed
1 cup Ricotta cheese
salt, pepper and grated
    nutmeg to taste
TO FINISH:
2/3 cup grated Parmesan
    cheese

Serves 4
Preparation time:
35 minutes
Cooking time:
1 hour
Freezing:
Recommended

1. Place the ingredients for the first filling in a pan and simmer for 25 minutes, until pulpy. Add salt and pepper.
2. Meanwhile, make the pancakes. Place the dry ingredients in a bowl and make a well in the center. Add the eggs and half of the milk, then gradually mix in the flour to make a smooth batter. Stir in the remaining milk and beat for 2–3 minutes. Alternatively, place half of the flour and the remaining ingredients in a blender or food processor and work for 30 seconds. Add the remaining flour and blend for 30 seconds.
3. Lightly oil a 7 inch heavy-based frying pan and place over a high heat. When hot, pour in enough batter to cover the base. Cook until the edge is golden and bubbles appear on the surface, then turn and cook the other side until golden. Turn onto a plate and cover while cooking the remaining batter, to make 14 pancakes.
4. To make the second filling, melt the butter in a pan, add the spinach, onion and garlic and cook for about 5 minutes, until wilted and just tender. Season with salt, pepper and nutmeg and stir in the cheese.
5. Lightly grease an 8 inch round deep cake pan and line the base and side with pancakes, cutting to fit.
6. Cover the base with a layer of the first filling, top with a pancake, sprinkle lightly with Parmesan, then cover with a layer of the second filling. Repeat the layers, finishing with a pancake.
7. Cover with greased foil and steam or boil for 1 hour.
8. Cut into wedges and serve with tomato sauce (see page 22) and broccoli.

ZUCCHINI AND RICE STREUDELS

Although it looks very fragile, filo pastry is in fact quite easy to use.

2 tablespoons butter
1¹/₃ cups grated zucchini
1 onion, chopped
1 clove garlic, crushed
1 cup brown rice, cooked
¹/₂ cup slivered almonds, toasted
1 egg, beaten

¹/₄ cup whipping cream
²/₃ cup grated Parmesan cheese
¹/₂ teaspoon dried thyme
8 sheets frozen filo pastry, thawed
sesame seeds for sprinkling
salt and pepper to taste

Serves 4
Preparation time:
45 minutes, plus chilling
Cooking time:
25 minutes
Freezing:
Recommended

1. Melt half of the butter in a pan, add the zucchini, onion and garlic, cover and cook for 5 minutes.
2. Transfer to a bowl, add the rice, almonds, egg, cream, Parmesan, thyme, and salt and pepper and mix well. Leave to cool, then chill for 30 minutes.
3. Melt the remaining butter. Allowing 2 sheets of filo pastry per streudel, brush one filo sheet with butter, then top with the other. Spread a quarter of the filling lengthways along one side of the filo, then roll up.
4. Brush the edges of the filo with butter to seal, then brush the streudel all over to glaze and roll loosely into a coil. Sprinkle with sesame seeds. Repeat with the remaining filo and filling.
5. Bake in a 375°F oven for 25 minutes. Serve hot with salad.

EGGPLANT PARMIGIANA

2 medium-size eggplants, sliced
7 tablespoons olive oil (approximately)
2 large onions, chopped
3–4 carrots, chopped
3 celery sticks, chopped
1 green pepper, cored, seeded and chopped
2 cloves garlic, crushed

2 teaspoons coriander seeds, crushed
1 teaspoon dried thyme
²/₃ cup red or white wine
2 × 14 oz cans chopped tomatoes
2 cups chopped Mozzarella cheese
1¹/₃ cups grated Parmesan cheese
salt and pepper to taste

1. Arrange the eggplant slices in layers in a colander, sprinkling each layer with salt. Leave to stand for about 30 minutes, then rinse and pat dry with paper towels.

2. Heat 5 tablespoons oil in a large frying pan and fry the eggplant in batches: brush the slices with oil as necessary, and add a little water to each batch; cook until softened. Drain on paper towels.

3. Heat another 2 tablespoons oil in the pan, add the vegetables and garlic and fry for 10 minutes. Add the coriander, thyme and wine and cook for 5 minutes. Add the tomatoes, season well with salt and pepper, cover and simmer for 20 minutes.

4. Arrange the eggplant slices, tomato sauce and cheeses in alternate layers in a 3 quart casserole dish, finishing with cheese; reserve a little of both cheeses.

5. Cover and cook in a 375°F oven for about 1 hour; uncover for the last 20 minutes and top with the reserved cheese.

6. Serve with crusty garlic bread and a green salad or green vegetables.

Serves 4
Preparation time:
40 minutes, plus standing time
Cooking time:
About 1 hour
Freezing:
Recommended

SOFT FRUIT COMPOTE WITH LIQUEUR CREAM

Don't blanch at the thought of eating flowers—these are quite harmless and look lovely.

1 lb mixed soft fruits, e.g. peaches, apricots, strawberries, kiwi fruit
3 tablespoons superfine sugar
3 tablespoons liqueur, e.g. Galliano, kirsch, Grand Marnier, Drambuie

grated rind and juice of 1 orange
1 egg white
2/3 cup heavy cream, whipped
borage or violet flowers (optional)

Serves 4
Preparation time: 15 minutes, plus standing
Freezing: Not recommended

1. Place the prepared fruits in a glass bowl; cut into spoon-size pieces if necessary. Sprinkle with the sugar, 1 tablespoon of the liqueur and the orange juice. Cover and leave for about 2 hours.
2. Whisk the egg white until stiff, then fold into the cream with the remaining liqueur and the orange rind.
3. Decorate the fruit with flowers, if you wish, and serve with the liqueur cream.

BROWN BREAD ICE CREAM

This is one of the oldest ice creams, originating in the
eighteenth century.

*2 cups fresh whole wheat
   breadcrumbs, toasted
6 egg yolks
¾ cup light brown
   sugar, packed*

*1¼ cups milk
1¼ cups whipping cream
1 teaspoon vanilla*

1. Crush the breadcrumbs with a rolling pin until fine.
2. Whisk the egg yolks and sugar together. Place the milk,
cream and vanilla in a pan and heat until almost boiling,
then pour from a height onto the egg yolks, whisking
constantly.
3. Return to a very low heat, stirring constantly, until the
thickness of whipping cream; do not allow to boil. Leave to
cool, then chill thoroughly.
4. Stir in the breadcrumbs, turn into a shallow freezerproof container, cover, seal and freeze for about 6–8
hours, until firm; stir occasionally during freezing.
5. Transfer to the refrigerator 20 minutes before serving
to soften. Scoop into glass dishes and serve with a fruit
compote, e.g. blackberry and apple, if you wish.

Serves 4
Preparation time:
10 minutes
Cooking time:
10 minutes
Freezing time:
6–8 hours

BANANAS WITH ORANGE AND RUM

*4 large ripe bananas,
   sliced thickly
grated rind and juice of
   1 large orange
2 tablespoons butter*

*2 tablespoons light brown
   sugar
2 tablespoons rum
ground cinnamon to
   sprinkle
chopped walnuts to serve*

Serves 4
Preparation time:
10 minutes
Cooking time:
15–20 minutes
Freezing:
Not recommended

1. Place the bananas in 4 ovenproof ramekins.
2. Place the orange rind and juice, butter and sugar in a pan and heat gently until melted, then stir in the rum.
3. Pour over the bananas, sprinkle with cinnamon and bake in a 350°F oven for 15–20 minutes, until just soft. Sprinkle with walnuts and serve warm.

RASPBERRY AND NUT MERINGUE

Prepare the meringue rounds and filling in advance, but assemble the gateau 1 hour before serving, to keep the meringue crisp.

*3 egg whites
3/4 cup light brown sugar,
   packed
3/4 cup finely ground
   filberts or walnuts*

*2 1/2 cups raspberries
1/2 cup cream cheese
1/2 cup low-fat ricotta
2 tablespoons powdered
   sugar*

Serves 4
Preparation time:
20 minutes
Cooking time:
40–50 minutes
Freezing:
Recommended for
meringue rounds
only

1. Cut 3 pieces of foil to fit baking sheets or upturned roasting pans and grease lightly.
2. Whisk the egg whites until stiff, then whisk in the sugar until smooth, glossy and very stiff. Fold in the ground nuts.
3. Spread into three 8 inch circles on the foil.
4. Bake in a 325°F oven for 40–50 minutes, until crisp on top; this may have to be done in batches.
5. Turn the meringues upside down on a rack and carefully peel off the foil in strips while warm.
6. Reserve a quarter of the raspberries. Place the rest in a blender or food processor with the soft cheeses and powdered sugar and work until smooth.
7. Sandwich the 3 meringues together with two thirds of the raspberry mixture. Spread the rest on the top and decorate with the reserved raspberries.

ITALIAN-STYLE DINNER FOR FOUR

This is a good 'prepare ahead' dinner—the main course simply needs rice or pasta to serve. If fresh peaches are unavailable for the sorbet, use canned ones in natural juice; use the juice instead of water in the recipe.

MENU

Peperonata with Prosciutto, Chicken with Fennel Ragù, Peach Sorbet with Fruit Coulis.

Suggested wines. *Appetizer:* Dry white wine or dry sherry. *Main course:* Dry red wine.

PEPERONATA WITH PROSCIUTTO

Peppers assume a delicious smoky flavor when broiled or roasted, which nicely complements the salty tang of prosciutto ham.

2 large red peppers
2 large green peppers
½ cup raisins
6 thin slices prosciutto
ham, halved lengthways
FOR THE DRESSING:
3 tablespoons olive oil

1 ½ tablespoons wine or
cider vinegar
1 clove garlic, crushed
1 teaspoon Dijon mustard
¼ teaspoon salt
black pepper to taste

Serves 4
Preparation time:
10 minutes, plus chilling
Cooking time:
30 minutes
Freezing:
Not recommended

1. Place the peppers on a baking sheet and roast in a 425°F oven for about 30 minutes, turning occasionally, until the skins start to blacken and blister. Leave to cool, then peel, core and slice. Place in a bowl with the raisins.
2. Whisk the dressing ingredients together, pour over the peppers and raisins and mix well. Cover and chill until required.
3. Roll up the ham slices and arrange on individual plates with the pepper and raisin salad.

CHICKEN WITH FENNEL RAGÙ

4 chicken quarters
whole wheat flour to coat
2 tablespoons olive oil
2 tablespoons butter
2 fennel, sliced
4 leeks, sliced thinly
1 clove garlic, crushed
1¼ cups dry white wine
¼ lb small mushrooms

15 oz can tomato sauce
1 tablespoon chopped
   marjoram
¼ cup chopped parsley
salt and pepper to taste
½ cup slivered almonds,
   toasted
fennel sprigs to garnish

Serves 4
Preparation time:
15 minutes
Cooking time:
About 50 minutes
Freezing:
Recommended

1. Coat the chicken in the flour. Heat the oil in a pan, add the chicken and fry until evenly browned. Set aside.

2. Add the butter, fennel, leek, garlic and 2 tablespoons water to the pan, cover and cook for 10–15 minutes.

3. Add the wine and simmer, uncovered, until reduced by half, then add mushrooms, tomato sauce, herbs, and salt and pepper. Return the chicken to the pan, cover and simmer gently for about 30 minutes until cooked.

4. Sprinkle with the almonds, garnish with fennel and serve with rice or pasta.

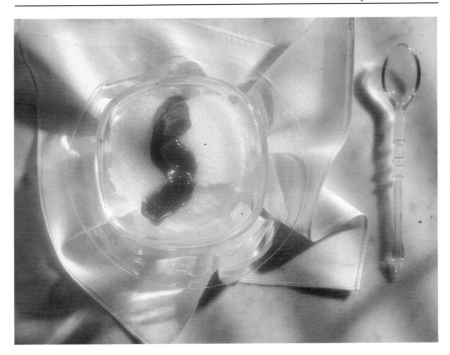

PEACH SORBET WITH FRUIT COULIS

1 lb peaches, skinned and pitted
grated rind and juice of 1 lemon
2 tablespoons brandy (optional)

½ cup sugar
1¼ cups water
1 cup raspberries
sugar to taste
strawberries or raspberries to serve (optional)

1. Place the peaches, lemon rind and juice, and brandy if using, in a blender or food processor and work until smooth.
2. Place the sugar and water in a pan and heat gently until dissolved, then boil for 5 minutes. Stir into the puree and leave to cool. Turn into a freezerproof container, cover, seal and freeze for about 2 hours, until partially frozen. Beat until slushy, then return to the freezer until firm.
3. Meanwhile, stew the raspberries with a little water and sugar to taste until soft and pulpy. Rub through a nylon sieve and leave to cool.
4. Transfer the sorbet to the refrigerator about 20 minutes before serving, to soften. Scoop into individual glass dishes and serve with the raspberry sauce, and strawberries or raspberries if wished.

Serves 4
Preparation time: 25 minutes
Freezing time: About 4 hours

EASTERN MEDITERRANEAN-STYLE DINNER FOR FOUR

The appetizer with its lovely colors should be a good talking point! Try and use a brightly colored melon such as Charentais or watermelon. The kebabs could be skewered ready to be broiled just before sitting down. Serve them with a colorful mixed salad, and rice or a garlic-buttered sesame seed loaf.

MENU
Feta and Melon Salad, Souvlakia, Rosewater Cherries.
Suggested wines. Retsina—an acquired taste, so serve a dry white wine as well.

FETA AND MELON SALAD

*1 small ripe melon or ¼
    watermelon
¼ lb mixed salad
    leaves*

*7 oz Feta cheese
12 small black olives
¼ cup vinaigrette dressing*

Serves 4
Preparation time:
20 minutes, plus
chilling
Freezing:
Not recommended

1. De-seed, peel and cut the melon into about 16 thin wedges.
2. Shred the salad leaves and arrange on 4 individual plates.
3. Cut the cheese into 16 fingers 1½ inches long.
4. Arrange the cheese, melon and olives around the salad. Trickle over the dressing and chill lightly before serving.

SOUVLAKIA

*1½ lb boned leg of lamb,
    cut into 1 inch cubes
1 onion, grated
¼ cup chopped parsley
juice of ½ lemon*

*1 teaspoon ground cumin
1 teaspoon paprika
1 onion, quartered
salt and pepper to taste*

Serves 4
Preparation time:
10 minutes, plus
marinating
Cooking time:
About 15 minutes
Freezing:
Recommended at
end of stage 2

1. Place all the ingredients, except the quartered onion, in a bowl, cover and leave to marinate for at least 2 hours. Remove the lamb with a slotted spoon.
2. Separate the onion quarters into segments and thread on 4 long skewers alternately with the meat.
3. Broil the kebabs for about 15 minutes, basting occasionally with the marinade, until tender. Serve with rice and a tomato and cucumber salad.

ROSEWATER CHERRIES

*1 lb fresh, or 15 oz can,
    black cherries, pitted*
*1 1/2 tablespoons triple
    strength rosewater*
*1/2 teaspoon ground
    ginger*

*1/2 teaspoon ground
    cinnamon*
1 tablespoon honey
*1 cup Greek strained
    yogurt*
*few unsalted pistachios,
    chopped*

1. If using fresh cherries, simmer with about ⅔ cup water and sugar to taste for about 5 minutes. If using canned cherries, drain off all but 2 tablespoons of the syrup.
2. Stir in the rosewater, then chill until required.
3. Stir the spices and honey into the yogurt.
4. Divide the cherries between individual serving dishes and top with the yogurt. Sprinkle with the chopped pistachios to serve.

Serves 4
Preparation time:
5–10 minutes, plus
chilling
Freezing:
Not recommended

FAR EASTERN-STYLE DINNER FOR FOUR

The saté and sea bass can be prepared ahead to the cooking stage, then finished off before the guests arrive. Sea bass has a superb flavor and texture, but is quite expensive; mullet, porgy or haddock could be substituted. Serve with rice, carrot julienne and stir-fried broccoli. If available, use jasmine flowers to decorate the dessert, for an effective finish.

MENU
Pork Saté, Chinese-baked Sea Bass, Lychee and China Tea Sorbet
Suggested wine: Dry white wine, or Jasmine tea if you prefer.

PORK SATÉ

*3/4 lb pork escalopes or
tenderloin
salt and pepper to taste
FOR THE MARINADE:
2 tablespoons fruit chutney
1 tablespoon soy sauce
2 tablespoons salad oil
1 teaspoon ground red
pepper
1/2 teaspoon ground
cumin*

*1 clove garlic, crushed
FOR THE SAUCE:
1/4 cup ground dry roasted
peanuts
1 clove garlic, crushed
3 tablespoons wine
vinegar
pinch of sugar
1 tablespoon water
TO SERVE:
shredded lettuce*

Serves 4
Preparation time:
10 minutes, plus
marinating
Cooking time:
6–8 minutes
Freezing:
Not recommended

1. Mix the marinade ingredients together in a dish.
2. Cut the escalopes in half lengthways; if using tenderloin, cut in half then slice each half lengthways to give 4 long slices. Add to the marinade, cover and chill for 4 hours.
3. Mix the sauce ingredients together in a bowl, then transfer to a small serving dish.
4. Remove the pork from the marinade with a slotted spoon and pleat onto 4 skewers. Season with salt and pepper and broil for 3–4 minutes on each side, until tender.
5. Arrange the shredded lettuce on 4 individual serving plates and place the kebabs on top. Serve immediately, accompanied by the saté sauce.

CHINESE-BAKED SEA BASS

*1 sea bass, weighing about
    2 lb, cleaned*
*2 teaspoons cornstarch
    blended with 1 cup fish
    stock or water*
*2 carrots, cut into julienne
    strips*
3 scallions, shredded
FOR THE MARINADE:
*2 tablespoons sunflower
    oil*

*1 teaspoon sesame oil
    (optional)*
*1 tablespoon shredded
    fresh root ginger*
3 scallions, sliced
*2 tablespoons light soy
    sauce*
pinch of sugar
salt to taste

Serves 4
Preparation time:
10 minutes, plus
marinating
Cooking time:
About 40 minutes
Freezing:
Not recommended

1. Make 3 slashes on each side of the fish and place on a large sheet of foil. Mix the marinade ingredients together, pour over the fish and rub well in. Fold the foil to form a parcel, sealing well, and leave to marinate for 2 hours.

2. Bake in a 350°F oven for about 40 minutes, until cooked and firm. Transfer the fish to a large warmed serving platter and keep warm. Drain the juices into a pan. Add the blended cornstarch and bring to the boil, stirring.

3. Add the carrots and onions and simmer for 2 minutes. Pour over the fish and serve immediately, with rice.

LYCHEE AND CHINA TEA SORBET

*1 lb lychees, peeled and
   pitted
2 Earl Grey or Jasmine tea
   bags
1 cup sugar*

*grated rind and juice of
   1 lemon
2 egg whites
jasmine flowers to
   decorate (optional)*

1. Puree the lychees in a blender or food processor. Strain, reserving the juice, and squeezing the pulp dry; you should have 1¼ cups juice.
2. Infuse the tea bags in 2½ cups boiling water for 10 minutes; remove the tea bags.
3. Dissolve the sugar in the tea, add the lemon rind and juice and simmer for 5 minutes. Leave to cool.
4. Mix in the lychee juice, then pour into a shallow freezerproof container, cover, seal and freeze for about 2 hours, until half-frozen and slushy.
5. Whisk the egg whites until soft peaks form. Beat the half-frozen puree to break down the ice crystals, then fold in the egg whites.
6. Cover, seal and freeze for 3 hours, until firm. Transfer to the refrigerator 20 minutes before serving, to soften. Decorate with jasmine flowers, if wished.

**Serves 4
Preparation time:**
30 minutes
Freezing time:
About 5 hours

SCANDINAVIAN-STYLE DINNER FOR SIX

An inexpensive meal that can all be prepared ahead. If you can't get herrings, use small mackerel, although they may be tricky to roll up. Serve the meatballs with a tomato salad, for color. Kissel can be served with cream.

MENU
Marinated Herrings, Pork Balls with Spinach Sauce, Kissel.
Suggested drinks. *Starter:* schnapps or vodka. *Main course:* try a full-flavored beer.

MARINATED HERRINGS

1 cup dry white wine
3 tablespoons wine or
cider vinegar
1 onion, sliced thinly
1 carrot, sliced
1 bayleaf

bouquet garni of thyme,
parsley and dill
6 small herrings, heads
removed and boned
juice of 1 small lemon
salt and pepper to taste
dill sprigs to garnish

Serves 6
Preparation time:
15 minutes, plus
marinating
Cooking time:
About 15 minutes
Freezing:
Recommended

1. Place the wine, vinegar, onion, carrot, bayleaf and bouquet garni in a pan and bring to the boil. Simmer, uncovered, for 5 minutes.
2. Meanwhile, season the flesh of the fish with salt and pepper and sprinkle with lemon juice. Roll up each herring from the neck to the tail and secure with a wooden cocktail stick.
3. Place the rolled herrings in a shallow ovenproof dish and pour over the wine mixture. Cover with foil and cook in a 425°F oven for about 15 minutes or until cooked. Leave in the marinade to cool overnight.
4. Remove the rolled herrings from the marinade with a slotted spoon and transfer to individual serving plates. Garnish with dill sprigs and serve with thinly sliced whole wheat bread.

Illustrated below
right: Pork Balls
with Spinach
Sauce (page 62)

PORK BALLS WITH SPINACH SAUCE

6 slices whole wheat bread,
 crusts removed
2/3 cup finely chopped
 bacon
1/3 cup chopped parsley
2 lb ground pork
1 egg, beaten
6 oz Gruyère or Swiss
 cheese, cut into 24 cubes
3 tablespoons salad oil
FOR THE SAUCE:
1 large onion, chopped
2 cloves garlic, crushed

1 teaspoon ground cumin
2 tablespoons whole wheat
 flour
3¾ cups chicken stock
1 lb spinach, stalks
 removed, shredded
2/3 cup sour cream
salt and pepper to taste
TO SERVE:
1 lb noodles, cooked
4 strips bacon, broiled
 crisply and chopped
parsley sprigs to garnish

Serves 6
Preparation time:
25 minutes
Cooking time:
20 minutes
Freezing:
Recommended

Illustrated on
page 61

1. Cover the bread with cold water and soak for 5 minutes, then squeeze dry.
2. Mix with the bacon, parsley, pork, egg, and salt and pepper.
3. With wet hands, divide and shape the mixture into 24 patties. Press a cheese cube into the center and re-form into balls.
4. Heat the oil in a pan, add the pork balls in batches and brown quickly. Transfer to a roasting pan and cook in a 375°F oven for 20 minutes.
5. Meanwhile make the sauce: add the onion and garlic to the pan and saute for about 5 minutes, to soften. Add the cumin and fry for 1 minute, then add the flour and fry for 1 minute.
6. Gradually stir in the stock and bring to the boil, stirring. Season with salt and pepper and add the spinach. Cover and simmer for 5 minutes.
7. Puree in a blender or food processor until smooth, then rub through a sieve to make a really smooth sauce. Reheat gently, whisking in the sour cream.
8. Transfer the pork balls to a plate lined with noodles. Pour over some sauce and sprinkle with the bacon. Garnish with parsley. Hand the remaining sauce separately.

KISSEL

For a traditional Kissel, the fruit is strained through a muslin cloth. I prefer to leave the fruit whole, rather than strain it—to keep the texture and fiber.

2¹/₂ cups raspberries
2¹/₂ cups redcurrants or
    blueberries
1¹/₄ cups water

¹/₂ cup sugar
3 tablespoons potato flour
    or arrowroot, blended
    with a little water

1. Place the fruit, water and sugar in a pan and cook gently for 10–15 minutes, until soft and pulpy.
2. Stir in the blended potato flour or arrowroot and bring back to the boil, stirring until thickened. Leave to cool, then spoon into glass dishes and chill until required.
3. Serve with cream and whole wheat honey cookies if wished.

Serves 6
Preparation time:
5 minutes, plus chilling
Cooking time:
10–15 minutes
Freezing:
Not recommended

SCOTTISH-STYLE DINNER FOR FOUR

The shrimp can be prepared ahead and cooked just before serving. The other two courses can be made beforehand. Serve the pheasant with creamed potatoes and turnips mixed together, and a green vegetable, such as Cabbage with Lemon and Caraway (page 76). Flummery is nice on its own, but is well complemented by a little fresh or stewed fruit.

MENU
Whisky Shrimp, Pheasant Salmis, Honey and Almond Flummery.
Suggested wines. *Appetizer:* Dry sherry if you wish—but a drink is not really required! *Main course:* A full red wine.

WHISKY SHRIMP

A quick and easy appetizer with a delicious flavor. If you can obtain fresh shrimp, so much the better. If not, use frozen shelled shrimp and defrost thoroughly before use.

2 tablespoons butter
1 small onion, chopped
1 lb medium-size
*   shelled shrimp*
2 tablespoons whisky

2 tablespoons chopped
*   parsley*
3 tablespoons sour cream
salt, pepper and ground
*   mace to taste*

Serves 4
Preparation time:
5 minutes
Cooking time:
10 minutes
Freezing:
Not recommended

1. Melt the butter in a pan, add the onion and saute for about 3 minutes.
2. Add the shrimp and heat gently for 2 minutes. Add the whisky and cook for 1 minute.
3. Add the parsley and sour cream and heat through gently. Season with salt, pepper and mace.
4. Transfer the shrimp with a slotted spoon to 4 individual serving plates. Simmer the sauce until reduced by a third, then spoon over the shrimp. Serve immediately, with thinly sliced whole wheat bread.

PHEASANT SALMIS

¼ cup olive oil	2 tablespoons flour
1 large or 2 small	3¾ cups chicken stock
pheasants	1¼ cups red wine
1 carrot and 1 small	1 teaspoon tomato paste
onion, chopped finely	bouquet garni of bayleaf,
2 celery sticks, chopped	thyme and parsley
¼ lb mushrooms, chopped	salt and pepper to taste
finely	watercress to garnish

Serves 4
Preparation time:
30 minutes
Cooking time:
45–55 minutes
Freezing:
Recommended

1. Rub 2 tablespoons of the oil over the pheasants and season with salt and pepper. Cook in a 400°F oven for 25 minutes.
2. Meanwhile, heat the remaining oil in a pan, add the vegetables and saute for 5 minutes. Stir in the flour and cook for 2 minutes. Add the remaining ingredients and bring to the boil, stirring. Simmer for 15 minutes.
3. Cut the pheasants in half along the backbone, or into quarters if using 1 large pheasant.
4. Strain the sauce over the pheasants and return to the oven for 20–30 minutes or until cooked. Garnish with watercress to serve.

HONEY AND ALMOND FLUMMERY

5 cups milk
6 tablespoons honey
1 cup ground almonds
1 teaspoon almond extract
2 teaspoons orange flower
  water

2 envelopes gelatin
6 tablespoons very hot
  water
TO DECORATE:
strips of orange rind or
  violet flowers

1. Place the milk, honey, ground almonds, almond extract and orange flower water in a pan and simmer for 2 minutes. Leave to cool.

2. Sprinkle the gelatin onto the hot water. and stir briskly until dissolved. Stir into the almond milk, then pour into 4 lightly oiled 1¼ cup molds and chill for about 6–8 hours, until set.

3. To turn out, dip the mold briefly into hot water and shake out onto a plate. Decorate with orange rind strips or violets. Serve with fresh raspberries or lightly stewed blackberries and apples, if you wish.

Serves 4
Preparation time:
5 minutes
Setting time:
About 6–8 hours
Freezing:
Not recommended

VALENTINE DINNER FOR TWO

The appetizer does need a little last-minute attention, but this can always be done together! If you can't find scallops, use jumbo shrimp instead. The other two courses can be prepared ahead. Serve the chicken with buttered parsley rice or pasta bows and a tomato (love apple) salad—with no garlic!

MENU
Scallop and Avocado Gratin, Declarations of Intent, Pink Passion Crush.
Suggested wines. Sparkling rosé or white wine or the best Champagne you can afford.

SCALLOP AND AVOCADO GRATIN

⅔ cup fish stock or water
⅔ cup dry white wine
1 small onion, sliced
1 bayleaf
6 peppercorns
6 scallops, sliced
8 small mushrooms
1 teaspoon cornstarch,
  blended with 1
  tablespoon water

2 tablespoons whipping
  cream
½ avocado, peeled and
  sliced
2 teaspoons grated
  Cheddar cheese
2 teaspoons dried
  breadcrumbs
salt to taste

Serves 2
Preparation time:
10 minutes
Cooking time:
15 minutes
Freezing:
Not recommended

1. Place the stock or water, wine, onion, bayleaf, peppercorns and salt in a pan and boil for about 7 minutes, until reduced to ⅔ cup.
2. Add the scallops and mushrooms, cover and cook gently for 3–4 minutes until tender. Transfer the scallops and mushrooms to 2 large ovenproof scallop shells with a slotted spoon, cover and keep warm.
3. Add the blended cornstarch to the stock, bring to the boil, stirring, then simmer for 1 minute, until thickened. Strain, then stir in the cream.
4. Arrange 2 or 3 avocado slices on each shell, pour over the sauce, cover and keep warm until required.
5. Sprinkle with the cheese and breadcrumbs and broil to brown. Serve immediately.

DECLARATIONS OF INTENT

2 boneless chicken breasts,
  each weighing 1/3 lb
  skinned
2 slices Parma ham
2 thin slices Gruyère cheese
1/2 leek, cut into thin strips
1/2 red pepper

2 tablespoons dry
  vermouth or sherry
2 tablespoons whipping
  cream (optional)
1 tablespoon butter
salt and pepper to taste

Serves 2
Preparation time:
10 minutes
Cooking time:
About 20 minutes
Freezing:
Not recommended

1. Slit the chicken breasts neatly in half horizontally. Insert the ham and cheese, close up and re-form.
2. Blanch the leek strips in boiling water for 1 minute; drain well. Set aside a few strips.
3. Place the remaining leek strips on 2 sheets of waxed paper and arrange the chicken on top.
4. Cut out 6 hearts from the pepper, using a cutter if you have one. Place on top of the chicken and form kisses, i.e. xxx, with the reserved leeks.
5. Season with salt and pepper, pour over the vermouth or sherry and cream, if using, and dot with the butter. Fold the paper over the chicken and twist the ends to form 'crackers'. If you wish, make foil 'bows' and attach to each end.
6. Place on a baking sheet and cook in a 350°F oven for about 20 minutes, until tender. Keep warm until required. Serve with buttered rice sprinkled with parsley, or pasta bows, and a tomato salad.

PINK PASSION CRUSH

2 cups strawberries
2 ripe passion fruit, halved
1 tablespoon superfine
  sugar (optional)

3 tablespoons heavy cream
1 egg white

Serves 2
Preparation time:
15 minutes, plus
chilling
Freezing:
Not recommended

1. Reserve 2 strawberries for decoration. Halve and mash the rest lightly—do not make too runny.
2. Scoop the passion fruit pulp into a small sieve and rub the juice through into the strawberries. Add the sugar if you wish.
3. Whip the cream and egg white separately until both are stiff, then fold lightly into the fruit mixture.
4. Pile into individual glass dishes and decorate with the reserved strawberries, halved. Chill until required. Serve with thin dessert biscuits.

SARDINE AND SESAME SEED ROLLS

These can be made up in advance and baked during the main course.

*4 slices whole wheat bread,
   crusts removed*
*4 oz can sardines in oil,
   drained and mashed*
1 scallion, chopped
1 tablespoon lemon juice
*1 teaspoon French
   mustard*

1 teaspoon chutney
3 anchovies, chopped
*2 tablespoons butter,
   melted*
2 teaspoons sesame seeds
pepper to taste

Serves 4
Preparation time:
15 minutes
Cooking time:
15 minutes
Freezing:
Not recommended

1. Roll the bread with a rolling pin until pliable.
2. Mix the sardines, scallion, lemon juice, mustard, chutney, anchovies and pepper together.
3. Spread on the bread, roll up firmly and cut each roll in half; secure with a wooden cocktail stick if necessary.
4. Brush with the butter, sprinkle with the sesame seeds and bake in a 400°F oven for 15 minutes. Serve hot.

BACON AND PARMESAN ROLLS

Make these ahead and bake during the main course.

*4 slices whole wheat bread,
   crusts removed*
*3 tablespoons butter,
   softened*
*1/2 cup grated Parmesan
   cheese*

*few drops Worcestershire
   sauce*
4 strips bacon, halved
pepper to taste

Serves 4
Preparation time:
10 minutes
Cooking time:
15 minutes
Freezing:
Not recommended

1. Roll the bread with a rolling pin until pliable.
2. Mix a third of the butter with two thirds of the cheese, the Worcestershire sauce and pepper.
3. Spread on the bread and lay 2 half bacon rashers on top. Roll up firmly and cut in half; secure with wooden cocktail sticks if necessary.
4. Spread the tops with the remaining butter and sprinkle with the remaining cheese. Bake in a 400°F oven for 15 minutes. Serve hot.

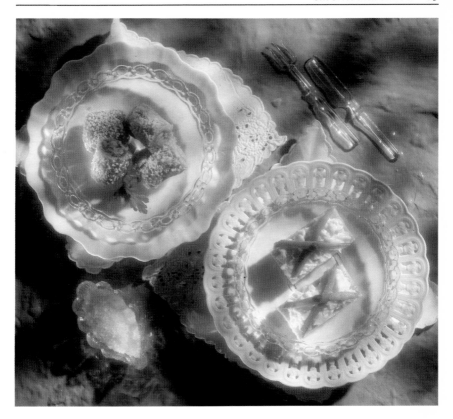

SCOTCH WOODCOCK

This has to be freshly cooked but the toast can be prepared beforehand.

4 slices bread, crusts removed, toasted
¼ cup butter
anchovy paste, to spread
4–6 eggs, beaten
salt, pepper and ground mace to taste

TO GARNISH:
4 anchovy fillets, halved lengthways
8 large capers, or chopped parsley

1. Spread the toast sparingly with some of the butter and a little anchovy paste. Cut in half lengthways and sandwich together. Place on 4 small warmed plates.
2. Melt the remaining butter in a small pan and scramble the eggs. Season with pepper, mace, and a little salt.
3. Pile on the toast and garnish with the anchovies in a cross and the capers or parsley. Serve immediately.

Serves 4
Preparation time: 10 minutes
Cooking time: 10 minutes
Freezing: Not recommended

ICED CHEESE

*8 oz just ripe Camembert,
Brie or Lymeswold
cheese
12 radishes with stalks
small bunch of black
grapes*

*4 small watercress sprigs
TO SERVE:
crackers, warmed
crushed ice*

Serves 4
Preparation time:
10 minutes
Freezing:
Not recommended

1. Line 4 freezerproof side plates with a bed of crushed ice and place in the freezer until required.
2. Cut the cheese into 4 slices and arrange on the ice about 10 minutes before serving.
3. Garnish the cheese with the remaining ingredients. Serve with the warm crackers, and butter if you wish.

GRILLED FETA CHEESE ON RYE

*4 slices rye bread with
caraway, toasted and
buttered lightly
8 slices feta cheese*

*1 tablespoon each chopped
dill and mint
1/2 small cucumber, cut
into sticks, to serve*

Serves 4
Preparation time:
3–5 minutes
Cooking time:
10 minutes
Freezing:
Not recommended

1. Cut the toast in half lengthways. Top with the cheese and broil for 3–5 minutes, until golden.
2. Sprinkle with the herbs and serve immediately, accompanied by the cucumber.

STILTON AND WATERCRESS WAFERS

These can be made up an hour or so before the meal.

*2 oz blue Stilton cheese,
derinded
1 tablespoon butter,
softened
1/2 bunch watercress, leaves
only, chopped*

*1 scallion, chopped
12 small crackers
TO GARNISH:
6 black olives, pitted and
halved, or 3 cherry
tomatoes, sliced*

Serves 4–6
Preparation time:
15 minutes
Freezing:
Not recommended

1. Mash the Stilton and butter together until smooth, then mix in the watercress and scallion.
2. Spread on the crackers, swirling attractively.
3. Garnish with the olives or tomatoes to serve.

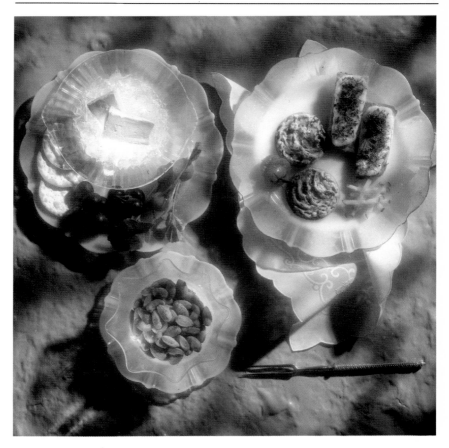

DEVILED NUTS

For after-meal nibbling. Prepare ahead and heat after the main course.

1 tablespoon butter
1 cup whole blanched
  almonds or unsalted
  cashews, or a mixture of
  both

good pinch of garlic salt
¹/₄ teaspoon ground red
  pepper
fine sea salt or crushed
  rock salt to sprinkle

1. Melt the butter in a pan and allow to go light brown. Immediately remove from the heat and pour over the nuts. Add the garlic salt and ground red pepper and mix well.
2. Spread on a baking sheet and bake in a 400°F oven for 15 minutes, shaking the nuts occasionally. Drain on paper towels.
3. Sprinkle with sea salt or rock salt and serve hot.

Serves 4
Preparation time:
5 minutes
Cooking time:
15 minutes
Freezing:
Not recommended

PEAS WITH LETTUCE

Serves 4–6
Preparation time:
10 minutes
Cooking time:
8 minutes
Freezing:
Not recommended

2/3 cup light stock
1 romaine lettuce, sliced
1 onion, sliced

4 cups frozen peas
1 tablespoon chopped mint
salt and pepper to taste

1. Place the stock in a large pan, add the lettuce and onion, cover and cook for 5 minutes.
2. Add the peas and mint and cook for 3 minutes. Season with salt and pepper and serve immediately.

CABBAGE WITH LEMON AND CARAWAY

Serves 4–6
Preparation time:
5 minutes
Cooking time:
About 5 minutes
Freezing:
Not recommended

1 small Chinese cabbage or
*   medium Savoy,*
*   shredded*
3 tablespoons butter

2 teaspoons caraway seeds
juice of 1 lemon
salt and pepper to taste

1. Boil or steam the cabbage for 3–5 minutes until just tender; drain.
2. Melt the butter in a small pan, add the caraway seeds and fry lightly for 1 minute. Add the lemon juice.
3. Toss into the cabbage, add salt and pepper and serve.

GREEN BEANS IN TOMATO CONCASSE

Any type of green bean is suitable for this dish. Top and tail, and string if necessary.

3 cups green beans
2 tablespoons olive oil
1 small onion, chopped
1/4 cup chopped cilantro
*   leaves*

4 medium-size tomatoes,
*   skinned, seeded and*
*   chopped*
salt and pepper to taste

Serves 4
Preparation time:
20 minutes
Cooking time:
6–9 minutes
Freezing:
Not recommended

1. Boil the beans in salted water for 5–8 minutes, according to taste; drain.
2. Meanwhile, heat the oil in a pan, add the onion and saute for 5 minutes. Add the cilantro and cook for 1 minute. Stir in the tomatoes and cook for 1 minute.
3. Toss into the beans, add salt and pepper and serve hot.

CARROTS SWEET AND SOUR

6–8 medium-size carrots,
  cut into julienne strips
5 scallions, shredded
2 thyme sprigs
1 teaspoon chopped fresh
  root ginger
1/2 teaspoon salt

2 tablespoons light brown
  sugar
1 tablespoon lemon or
  lime juice
pepper to taste
chopped parsley to serve

Serves 4–6
Preparation time:
10 minutes
Cooking time:
10–15 minutes
Freezing:
Recommended

1. Place all the ingredients in a pan, add enough water just to cover and simmer, uncovered, for 10–15 minutes, until all the liquid has evaporated.
2. Garnish with parsley to serve.

POTATOES BOULANGÈRE

2 lb potatoes, sliced thinly
1 large onion, sliced thinly
2 1/2 cups light stock

2 tablespoons butter,
  melted
salt, pepper and grated
  nutmeg to taste

Serves 6
Preparation time:
20 minutes
Cooking time:
About 1 1/2 hours
Freezing:
Not recommended

1. Layer the potato and onion slices in a shallow casserole, seasoning the layers well with salt, pepper and nutmeg. Finish with potato slices.
2. Pour in the stock and brush potatoes with the butter. Cook in a 350°F oven for about 1 1/2 hours, until cooked and crisp on top. Serve hot.

CREAMED SPROUTS

2 lb Brussels sprouts
1/2 cup curd cheese or
  farmer's cheese
salt, pepper and grated
  nutmeg to taste

2 tablespoons slivered
  almonds, toasted, to
  serve

Serves 6
Preparation time:
10 minutes
Cooking time:
About 10 minutes
Freezing:
Not recommended

1. Boil the sprouts in salted water for about 10 minutes, until just tender. Drain, reserving a little water.
2. Place half of the sprouts and cheese in a food processor or blender and work until smooth. Transfer to a warmed serving dish. Repeat with remaining sprouts and cheese.
3. Add a little of the reserved cooking liquid if the puree is too dry. Season with salt, pepper and nutmeg.
4. Sprinkle with the almonds to serve.

BABY RÖSTI

1 lb small potatoes, halved
1/3 lb parsnips or turnips,
   cut into 2 inch pieces
3 scallions, sliced
   thinly

1 clove garlic, crushed
2 tablespoons butter
3 tablespoons salad oil
salt, pepper and ground
   mace to taste

Makes about 6
Preparation time:
15 minutes
Cooking time:
About 20 minutes
Freezing:
Recommended

1. Cook the potato and parsnip or turnip in boiling salted water for 8 minutes. Leave to cool, then grate coarsely into a bowl. Add the scallions, garlic, and salt, pepper and mace and mix well.
2. Heat half of the butter and oil in a heavy-based frying pan and add half of the potato mixture. Using a 3 inch cutter, press into 3 patties in the pan; do not cook with the cutter in position.
3. Cook for about 5 minutes, until browned, then turn and cook the other side for about 5 minutes. Keep warm, uncovered, in a low oven while cooking the remaining mixture. Serve hot.

BROWN RICE WITH BROCCOLI, CELERY AND NUTS

1 cup brown rice
2 1/2 cups light stock
1 tablespoon butter
1/2 lb broccoli florets
3 tablespoons sunflower
   oil
1 clove garlic, crushed
2 celery sticks, sliced
   diagonally

4 scallions, sliced
   diagonally
2 tablespoons soy sauce
salt and pepper to taste
1/4 cup filberts or
   slivered almonds,
   toasted, to garnish
   (optional)

Serves 4
Preparation time:
15 minutes
Cooking time:
30 minutes
Freezing:
Recommended

1. Place the rice and stock in a pan, cover and simmer gently for 30 minutes. Add the butter.
2. Meanwhile, break the broccoli into small pieces and slice the stalks if necessary.
3. Toward the end of the rice cooking time, heat the oil and garlic in a pan, add the vegetables and stir-fry for about 5 minutes. Add the soy sauce and salt and pepper.
4. Stir into the rice and garnish with the nuts, if you wish.

VEGETABLE PUREES

Not an idea for coping with soggy or stale vegetables, but a delicious way of serving fresh ones. You will need a food processor, blender or large food mill.

Boil or steam as usual, seasoned or unseasoned, until just tender; do not overcook or the puree will be runny. Drain very well, then puree in a food processor or blender or rub through a food mill until smooth, but still thick enough to hold its shape. Add about 3 tablespoons cream, yogurt, soft butter or cooking water for every lb of vegetables. Season with salt and pepper and add a flavoring if you wish. The following suggestions go well together:

- Brussels sprouts with grated nutmeg or ground mace
- Carrots with chopped thyme, ground ginger or ground coriander
- Parsnips with mild curry powder and pine nuts
- Peas with chopped mint
- Turnips with grated orange rind
- Beet with horseradish relish
- Cauliflower with chopped tarragon and lemon juice

An attractive serving idea is to make up two contrasting color purees and pipe them in alternate stripes on a serving platter. Sprinkle with chopped herbs or toasted almonds, pine nuts or sesame seeds, if you wish.

Purees can be made ahead and reheated when required.

SIDE SALADS

Salads are a good dinner accompaniment—they can be prepared up to 24 hours ahead and kept bagged up and chilled. Do not dress leafy vegetables until ready to serve. Sliced tomatoes, grated raw carrots, and Waldorf-type salads can be dressed about 2 hours beforehand. Cold potato, rice and pasta salads should be tossed with vinaigrette while still hot, then mixed with other ingredients when cold.

Many new varieties of green salad vegetables are now available for much of the year and make an attractive feature on the table. Try and mix about three leafy vegetables, such as endive, shredded romaine lettuce, radicchio, young spinach, mâche and oakleaf lettuce. Add thinly sliced cucumber, Belgium endive or celery and sprinkle with chopped herbs. Pour over a well flavored vinaigrette or creamy dressing just before serving and toss at the table. Scatter on some toasted almonds for crunch.

Adventurous gardeners may like to grow sorrel, purslane or arugola, or allow some dandelion plants to thrive and pick the young leaves to add to salads. Nasturtium leaves and flowers add a peppery flavor. Other leafy salad herbs include borage, salad burnet and Good King Henry.

An attractive presentation for all leafy or mixed salads is to layer them in a glass bowl. Put springy leaf vegetables at the base, then add the heavier ingredients. Finish with a layer of sliced tomato, radish or carrot, or some edible flowers like nasturtium or borage.

INDEX

Photography by: Andy Seymour
Designed by: Sue Storey
Home economist: Carole Handslip
Stylist: Penny Legg
Illustration by: Linda Smith